GUIDE
to the
National Parks

by Elizabeth Krych

Scholastic Inc.
New York   Toronto   London   Auckland
Sydney   Mexico City   New Delhi   Hong Kong

For Rachel, with sisterhood from sea to shining sea

Photo Credits

CONTENTS

America the Beautiful

The lands that became the United States of America have always been extraordinary. From the Atlantic to the Pacific are all kinds of natural wonders!

In the 1800s, as lands were developed into farms, ranches, and towns, many Americans became dismayed by the destruction of America's natural beauty. The government began setting aside areas as protected public land. In 1872, Yellowstone National Park became the first national park in the world. In the twentieth century, hundreds more places were named protected national sites. Some of them were protected because of their environmental or historical value, not just their natural beauty.

The **National Park Service** was created in 1916 to oversee the parks. During the 1930s, over three million men joined the **Civilian Conservation Corps (CCC)** and worked to improve the parks. Today, **park rangers** maintain and protect the national parks from destruction.

For twelve years, from 2010 to 2021, the **U.S. Mint** will be honoring the diversity of America's landscape and history with special quarters. Each newly designed 25¢ coin will feature a different national park or public space important to America's legacy. Let's learn about America's amazing places!

HOT SPRINGS

National Park

Year of Quarter: 2010
Location of Park: Arkansas
Date of Park's Founding: 1832
Approximate Park Area: 5,500 acres
Fun Fact: Until the 1940s, many professional baseball teams did their spring training at Hot Springs.

Bathhouse Row contains eight of the fanciest hotels and spas of its time, built around the hot springs.

Would you enjoy taking a bath outside? Before most homes had running water, people traveled to a place in Arkansas where naturally heated springwater bubbles out of the ground. They believed the minerals dissolved in the water could cure pain and illness.

The historic buildings have beautiful statues and fountains.

President Andrew Jackson made this area the first national "reservation" in 1832, long before the national parks system existed. Elegant hotels built for visitors a hundred years ago are now part of the park.

The hot springs water is 143°F.

YELLOWSTONE

National Park

Year of Quarter: 2010
Location of Park: Wyoming, Montana, and Idaho
Date of Park's Founding: 1872
Approximate Park Area: 2,200,000 acres
Fun Fact: President Gerald Ford worked as a ranger at Yellowstone as a young man.

Old Faithful is the most famous of the park's more than 300 geysers.

Yellowstone was the world's first national park, chosen for its amazing hot springs, bubbling mud pots, and **geysers**. These jets of boiling water start deep beneath the surface, heated by the magma from an old volcano.

About 4,000 bison live in the park.

The most famous geyser, Old Faithful, is named for its frequent bursts.

Now that much of the West has been settled, Yellowstone's rugged landscape is one of the best places to spot moose, bison, elk, wolves, and grizzly bears. Protecting wildlife from the park's millions of visitors is a tough job for the park's rangers. In 1988, several fires, some started by human carelessness, burned 36 percent of the park.

The colors of hot springs such as Morning Glory Pool are caused by tiny creatures that live in the warm water.

The grizzly bear is listed as a threatened species in the U.S. There are approximately 500 grizzlies in Yellowstone park today.

YOSEMITE

National Park

Year of Quarter: 2010
Location of Park: California
Date of Park's Founding: 1890
Approximate Park Area: 760,000 acres
Fun Fact: The **sequoia** tree called the Grizzly Giant is 209 feet tall. That's as tall as 36 park rangers!

From the floor of Yosemite Valley, visitors can view majestic Cathedral Rocks and other cliffs and peaks.

Yosemite is a park of big things. Melting snow creates huge waterfalls that cascade down hundreds of feet. Soaring sequoia trees seem to grow up to the clouds. Sheer granite cliffs like El Capitan rise above deep, peaceful valleys.

Visitors to this popular national park in California come to see nature at its most magnificent, and enjoy camping and hiking among its beautiful scenery all year round.

Yosemite's mountains can also be seen on skis, or from a glider!

GRAND CANYON

National Park

Year of Quarter: 2010
Location of Park: Arizona
Date of Park's Founding: 1893
Approximate Park Area: 1,200,000 acres
Fun Fact: While the North Rim can get as much as 200 inches of snow a year, barely any snow ever reaches the canyon bottom!

Trails along the canyon rim and the long trek to the bottom are popular with hikers.

Carved by millions of years of Colorado River water, the Grand Canyon cuts a 277-mile-long gash through many levels of rock. The canyon reveals millions of years of rock layers stacked like a layer cake. Most of the canyon is over a mile deep. The width varies from ten to eighteen miles. Native Americans lived along the canyon in caves or stone houses for thousands of years. Today, visitors can explore the canyon's rocks and wildlife by hiking or rafting.

The desert horned lizard is one of many lizards and snakes in the park.

MOUNT HOOD

National Forest

Year of Quarter: 2010
Location of Park: Oregon
Date of Park's Founding: 1893 (as part of Cascade Range Forest Reserve); separated in 1908 and renamed in 1924
Approximate Park Area: 1,000,000 acres
Fun Fact: Mount Hood National Forest lands include the last segment of the Oregon Trail, the route that thousands of settlers took by covered wagon from the East in the 1800s.

Snowmelt and rainwater tumbles over 600 feet down Multnomah Falls.

It may look chilly now, but beneath the snowy slopes of Mount Hood and its blanket of evergreen trees is a dormant volcano. This wooded mountain area near Portland preserves a clean **watershed** for the city and allows hiking, skiing, berry picking, and even Christmas tree cutting! Its Timberline Lodge, a hotel built in 1936, is considered one of the finest buildings created by the CCC program (see page 4).

Snowy winters make the forest a favorite place for cross-country skiing.

GETTYSBURG

National Military Park

Year of Quarter: 2011

Location of Park: Pennsylvania

Date of Park's Founding: 1863 (as military cemetery); 1895 (as federal military park)

Approximate Park Area: 6,000 acres

Fun Fact: Painted in the 1880s, the Gettysburg Cyclorama is a wraparound painting that puts the viewer in the middle of the battle action. Stretched out, it would be longer than a football field!

Many monuments in the park memorialize the thousands of soldiers who died here, as well as President Lincoln's hope for peace. (bottom right)

In July 1863, the midpoint of the Civil War, a huge battle raged for three days across the farms, fields, and woods of central Pennsylvania. More than 51,000 American soldiers from the North and the South died, and the battlefield became a cemetery and memorial park. President Abraham Lincoln attended the dedication in November 1863, where he gave his famous speech, the Gettysburg Address: "Government of the people, by the people, for the people, shall not perish from the earth."

Lincoln's Address at the Dedication of the Gettysburg National Cemetery. November 19, 1863.

GLACIER

National Park

Year of Quarter: 2011
Location of Park: Montana
Date of Park's Founding: 1910
Approximate Park Area: 1,000,000 acres
Fun Fact: At the northern border of the United States, Glacier National Park was joined with Waterton Lakes National Park in Canada as the world's first International Peace Park in 1932.

Many big creatures live at Glacier Park, including mountain lions (upper left), gray wolves, elk, and grizzly bears.

Brr! Thousands of years ago, during the last **ice age**, North America was covered with moving sheets of ice called glaciers. When the global temperature started to warm up around 8,000 BCE, the glaciers retreated northward, shaping the landscape and leaving behind trails of crunched-up rocks. The remains of ancient glaciers are still stranded on granite peaks in this park in northern Montana, but hurry! Scientists predict that because of climate change, they all may be melted by 2020.

Crevice at Grinnell Glacier

OLYMPIC

National Park

Year of Quarter: 2011
Location of Park: Washington
Date of Park's Founding: 1897 (as Olympic Forest Preserve); 1938 expanded to Olympic National Park; coastline area added 1953
Approximate Park Area: 920,000 acres
Fun Fact: Washington State's Mount Olympus, 7,980 feet high, was named for the home of the gods in Greek mythology, as were the Olympic Games.

High mountain peaks have rushing rivers and large forests of pine trees.

The rainy forests of the lower parts of the park are home to the colorful Pacific tree frog.

Olympic Park's varied landscape is like three parks in one. Spread over nearly a million acres, it has ocean coast, temperate (moderate) rain forest, and subalpine (cold and steep) **ecosystems**. Playful otters and seals frolic in the waves along the Pacific shore. Along mossy forest trails, you can get up close to huge cedar trees. On a clear day, you can view the snowy peaks of the Olympic Mountains, which are frozen all year long.

Sea lions visit the rugged Pacific coastline of the park from late summer to early spring.

VICKSBURG

National Military Park

Year of Quarter: 2011
Location of Park: Mississippi and Louisiana
Date of Park's Founding: 1899
Approximate Park Area: 1,800 acres
Fun Fact: A colony of over 30 hoary bats lives in the roof of the Illinois Memorial.

Impressive memorials made of bronze and stone were donated by states in memory of soldiers who were injured or killed in the Battle of Vicksburg. Union General Ulysses S. Grant (bottom right) later became president.

After a **siege** of 47 days, Union General Ulysses S. Grant accepted the surrender of the key Confederate port of Vicksburg on July 4, 1863. Over time, hundreds of monuments and graves were built, marking the terrible human cost to both sides in this key battle of the Civil War. Visitors can also see a restored Union gunboat, the USS *Cairo*, which was preserved in Mississippi River mud for a hundred years before being recovered.

CHICKASAW

National Recreation Area

Year of Quarter: 2011

Location of Park: Oklahoma

Date of Park's Founding: 1902 (as Sulphur Springs Reservation); 1906 (as Platt National Park); expanded and renamed 1976

Approximate Park Area: 9,900 acres

Fun Fact: Platt National Park, the smallest national park until 1976, was absorbed into the recreation area.

Lake of the Arbuckles, popular for boating and fishing, is a man-made lake created in 1966.

This popular area of lakes, mineral springs, and nature trails is named for the Chickasaw Nation of Native Americans, who originally lived in the southeastern states, but was moved to this part of Indian Territory, now Oklahoma, in 1837. The tribe sold the land back to the U.S. government in 1902 in order to protect its mineral springs and other resources.

Lincoln Bridge (above) dates from 1909.

Bison have not lived wild in this area since the late 1800s, but a small, protected herd was brought to the park in 1920.

EL YUNQUE

National Forest

Year of Quarter: 2012
Location of Park: Puerto Rico
Date of Park's Founding: 1903
Approximate Park Area: 28,000 acres
Fun Fact: The Puerto Rican parrot, found in El Yunque Forest, is one of the rarest birds left in the wild.

Draped across the Luquillo Mountains in the eastern part of Puerto Rico, the forest is warm and rainy year-round.

El Yunque Forest was set aside as a nature preserve while Puerto Rico was still a Spanish colony. After the United States gained authority over the island, the forest remained protected. It's the only tropical forest in the U.S. national forest system. Many Puerto Ricans as well as visitors from cruise ships enjoy its tropical forest landscape, home to many rare and beautiful birds, flowers, and frogs.

CHACO CULTURE

National Historical Park

Year of Quarter: 2012

Location of Park: New Mexico

Date of Park's Founding: 1907 (as National Monument); 1980 (as National Historical Park)

Approximate Park Area: 34,000 acres

Fun Fact: Archaeological remains of chocolate have been found in 1,000-year-old jars at the Pueblo Bonita site. It probably came all the way from present-day Mexico!

The largest ruin is called Pueblo Bonita. It was once a huge, semicircular community center for the Chaco people.

A great town or trading post built of stone once flourished in northwest New Mexico, where the Chaco people gathered for trade or religious ceremonies. Archaeologists may never fully understand the purpose of the huge buildings or how they were built, but their complex designs may line up with star patterns. The site was abandoned by the Chaco in the 1200s, but its ruins remain a sacred place for many tribes of the Southwest.

Thousand-year-old petroglyphs, or "drawings on stone"

ACADIA

National Park

Year of Quarter: 2012

Location of Park: Maine

Date of Park's Founding: 1916 (as Sieur de Monts National Monument); 1919 (as Lafayette National Park); 1929 as Acadia National Park

Approximate Park Area: 47,000 acres

Fun Fact: Granite marking stones along the original roads are called Rockerfeller's Teeth after their donor, John Rockerfeller Jr.

The rocky Atlantic coast of Maine is popular for hiking and sailing.

Blueberry picking in summer, ice fishing in winter—this pretty part of Maine is welcoming to visitors all year round. The first national park east of the Mississippi is made up of islands and coastline donated by wealthy citizens in the early twentieth century. On Mount Desert Island, what used to be a private vacation area for rich families can now be enjoyed by everyone.

Bass Harbor Head Lighthouse, Mount Desert Island

HAWAI'I VOLCANOES

National Park

Year of Quarter: 2012
Location of Park: Hawai'i
Date of Park's Founding: 1916
Approximate Park Area: 320,000 acres
(But, with lava flow, getting bigger all
the time!)
Fun Fact: Measured from the sea floor,
volcanic Mauna Loa is taller than Mount
Everest!

Steam rises where hot, flowing
lava meets the ocean.

This park is hot, hot, hot! The
spectacular main attraction at
this unusual park is Mount
Kiluea, an active volcano that
has been erupting steadily since
1983. Oozing melted lava slides
down from the crater or vents to
the ocean, where it
cools and forms new land. Careful hikers can
watch eruptions from a safe distance. The park
also shelters endangered species of turtles and
waterbirds.

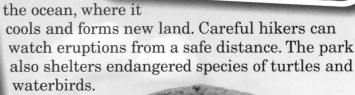

Green sea turtles
are protected
within the park.

DENALI

National Park and Preserve

Year of Quarter: 2012
Location of Park: Alaska
Date of Park's Founding: 1917
(as Mount McKinley National Park);
1980 expanded and renamed
Approximate Park Area: 6,100,000 acres
Fun Fact: The park and preserve lands are
larger than the individual areas of five
states: New Hampshire, New Jersey,
Connecticut, Delaware, and Rhode Island.

Wild Dall sheep (right) and tame sled dogs (bottom right) have thick fur to protect them through the harsh winters, which often go below -50°F.

Denali means "the High One" in the native Athapaskan language, while the English name for the park's famous peak is Mount McKinley, after the twenty-fifth president, William McKinley. Whatever you call it, it's the tallest mountain in North America!

Denali National Park has only one main road and is covered by snow for much of the year, so park rangers get around its huge area by dogsled, snowmobile, plane, and helicopter.

WHITE MOUNTAIN

National Forest

Year of Quarter: 2013
Location of Park: New Hampshire and Maine
Date of Park's Founding: 1918
Approximate Park Area: 800,000 acres
Fun Fact: Mount Washington is the tallest peak in the northeastern United States.

After a hundred years, trees have grown back and wildlife such as black bears have returned to the area.

By the early twentieth century, many people began to worry that America's woodlands were going to be lost forever. Entire forests were being cut down to be used for building and making paper. A 1911 law, the **Weeks Act**, allowed

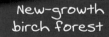

New-growth birch forest

national forests to be established where trees had been cut down. A century later, the spruce and birch trees in this mountainous part of New England have grown back and are protected for the future.

21

PERRY'S VICTORY

and International Peace Memorial

Year of Quarter: 2013
Location of Park: Ohio
Date of Park's Founding: 1919
Approximate Park Area: 25 acres
Fun Fact: The 352-foot monument is the tallest column of its kind in the world.

Six British and American officers killed in the Battle of Lake Erie are buried beneath the monument, but not Perry, whose grave is in Rhode Island.

"Don't Give Up the Ship!" said the flag of USS *Niagara* on September 10, 1813; on this day Oliver Perry led American battleships to victory over the British Navy in the Battle of Lake Erie, a turning point in the War of 1812. The century of peace among America, England, and Canada that followed was symbolized by a tall column built on South Bass Island in 1915, near the battle site.

Commodore Oliver Perry, 1785–1819

GREAT BASIN

National Park

Year of Quarter: 2013
Location of Park: Nevada
Date of Park's Founding: 1922
(as Lehman Caves National Monument);
1986 expanded and renamed
Approximate Park Area: 77,000 acres
Fun Fact: Some of the bristlecone pine
trees on Wheeler Peak are the oldest
living trees on Earth!

Park rangers lead tours of the amazing Lehman Caves.

A desert between two high mountain ranges, the Great Basin region in the West is a dry but lively place. Native American farmers, Basque shepherds from Spain, and gold prospectors from the eastern states have all settled here.

Today, visitors to the park can explore the Lehman Caves, carved by ancient rivers. Because the park is so far from bright city lights, it's one of the best places in the continental U.S. to stargaze.

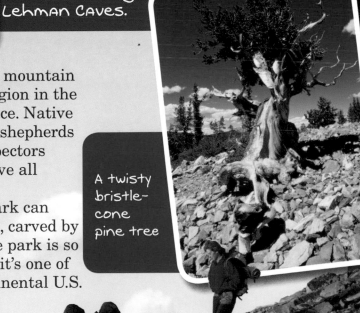

A twisty bristle-cone pine tree

FORT MCHENRY

National Monument and Historic Shrine

Year of Quarter: 2013
Location of Park: Maryland
Date of Park's Founding: 1925
Approximate Park Area: 43 acres
Fun Fact: Like the stars on the American flag, the island fort is shaped like a five-pointed star.

An artist's idea of Francis Scott Key (1779–1843) viewing the battle in 1812

A view from above shows the fort's five-pointed shape, which made it easier to defend from all sides.

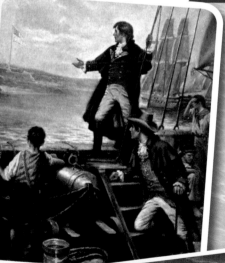

O say, can you see? On this island in Baltimore Harbor, a nighttime battle raged between British and American forces on September 14, 1814. An American lawyer, Francis Scott Key, watched as the island fort was shelled by explosives that lit up the sky but didn't overcome its defenses. He was inspired to write a poem that was later set to music and became our national anthem, "The Star-Spangled Banner." (*Spangled* means "decorated with.")

This statue of Orpheus, the musician of Greek mythology, commemorates the writing of "The Star-Spangled Banner."

MOUNT RUSHMORE

National Memorial

Year of Quarter: 2013

Location of Park: South Dakota

Date of Park's Founding: 1925

Approximate Park Area: 1,300 acres

Fun Fact: President Teddy Roosevelt's granite mustache is as long as 40 teddy bears (20 feet)!

It took 14 years for a team of workers to build the memorial, using dynamite, jackhammers, and hand tools.

In the 1920s, a South Dakota historian had the idea of creating a tourist attraction in the Black Hills. Nearly a hundred years later, his idea has succeeded beyond his wildest dreams! Millions of people come to South Dakota every year to see the faces of four great presidents carved into the granite rock face: George Washington, Thomas Jefferson, Theodore Roosevelt, and Abraham Lincoln. The massive project, completed in 1941, was led by sculptors Gutzon and Lincoln Borglum.

GREAT SMOKY MOUNTAINS

National Park

Year of Quarter: 2014
Location of Park: Tennessee and North Carolina
Date of Park's Founding: 1926
Approximate Park Area: 520,000 acres
Fun Fact: The "smoke" of the Great Smoky Mountains is actually mist formed by a natural chemical evaporating from millions of leafy trees.

More kinds of trees live amid the rolling hills here than in any other national park.

The nation's busiest national park is also one of the easiest to visit; it's free to drive through, but much more detail can be seen on foot. Hiking the park's many hilly trails reveals hidden waterfalls and mountain views, and wildlife including black bears and elk.

The temperate and rainy Great Smoky Mountains were originally the lands of the Cherokee Nation. Abandoned mountain farms and mills show how white settlers lived in these mountains before it became a park.

Mingus Mill, once used to grind cornmeal

SHENANDOAH

National Park

Year of Quarter: 2014
Location of Park: Virginia
Date of Park's Founding: 1926
Approximate Park Area: 200,000 acres
Fun Fact: President Herbert Hoover's summer home and fishing lodge, Rapidan Camp, is now within the park's land, and is open to visitors.

This park's mountain views make it a favorite place for hikers.

This rambling stretch of the Blue Ridge Mountains contains 101 miles of the Appalachian Trail, the hiking path that reaches over 2,000 miles from Georgia to Maine. Unlike most other national parks, the land that makes up Shenandoah Park was previously privately owned, and generations farmed and built their homes here. In the 1930s, CCC workers enhanced the park lands with scenic roadways and public buildings (see page 4).

A scarlet tanager, a treetop bird

ARCHES

National Park

Year of Quarter: 2014
Location of Park: Utah
Date of Park's Founding: 1929
(as Arches National Monument);
1971 (as national park)
Approximate Park Area: 77,000 acres
Fun Fact: The park's biggest
natural span, Landscape Arch,
is 306 feet wide!

Delicate Arch is one of many mysterious and beautiful rock formations left behind by water erosion.

Looking around the stony, crusty desert landscape of Arches today, it's hard to believe that this park was once covered by an ocean! But over millions of years,

Cacti and tiny kangaroo rats can both be found in the desert environment.

the action of water and ice here built up a thick layer of sandstone. Then it wore this down and broke up the rock, leaving behind more than 2,000 freestanding arches, balanced rocks, "windows," "fins," and pointy features called spires. Some famous rocks include Delicate Arch, Marching Men, and Double O Arch.

GREAT SAND DUNES

National Park and Preserve

Year of Quarter: 2014
Location of Park: Colorado
Date of Park's Founding: 1932 (as Great Sand Dunes National Monument); 2000 (as park and preserve)
Approximate Park Area: 150,000 acres
Fun Fact: Park visitors are welcome to sled or "sandboard" down the dunes!

Many species of birds stop off in the park lands during their migrations, including thousands of sandhill cranes (bottom right).

The name says it all: This park's main attraction is a group of the biggest sand dunes in the country. Hundreds of miles from any present-day ocean, the park's dunes are made up of sand left behind when a big lake dried up thousands of years ago. Wind funnels through mountain passes from the east and west and blows the dunes back and forth, but keeps them basically in the same place over time.

Surf's up, dude! A sandboarder surfs the dunes.

EVERGLADES

National Park

Year of Quarter: 2014
Location of Park: Florida
Date of Park's Founding: 1934
Approximate Park Area: 1,400,000 acres
Fun Fact: What are those eyes peeping out of the water—a crocodile or an alligator? This park has both!

Everglades was the first national park created to protect animals and plants, not just because the scenery was pretty.

Gentle manatees swim through the warm Everglades waters . . .

Wetlands once covered most of the Florida peninsula, a "river of grass" that slowly drained into the Gulf of Mexico. After much of this ecosystem was destroyed by human development, Everglades National Park was set aside at the southern tip of the state as a last sanctuary for the wildlife that depend on this unique habitat. Majestic birds such as spoonbills, ibises, and egrets glide above the marshy surface, while alligators, panthers, and crocodiles hunt for prey in the water and on the land.

. . . and so do fierce alligators!

HOMESTEAD

National Monument of America

Year of Quarter: 2015

Location of Park: Nebraska

Date of Park's Founding: 1936

Approximate Park Area: 210 acres

Fun Fact: Famous descendants of homesteaders include author Laura Ingalls Wilder, astronaut Bill Nelson, and actress Whoopi Goldberg.

Homesteaders usually lived in very simple cabins (left). The one-room prairie schoolhouse on the park site (below) enabled farm children to learn for nearly one hundred years.

The 1862 Homestead Act gave parcels of federally owned western land to anyone willing to develop it. People came from the eastern states and around the world to claim land and build new farms. Before the process ended in 1986, over a billion acres of land were earned by hardworking **homesteaders.**

On the site of the first claim, a heritage center and restored prairie land show what life was like for the very first homesteader, Daniel Freeman, and his family.

KISATCHIE

National Forest

Year of Quarter: 2015
Location of Park: Louisiana
Date of Park's Founding: 1936
Approximate Park Area: 600,000 acres
Fun Fact: In 1914, more timber was logged in Louisiana than in any other state.

After being heavily logged in the 1920s (below), the restored habitat of Kisatchie Forest is again home to the pine snake (lower right).

Named for a tribe that once lived in the area, Kisatchie Forest is a great success story of the national forest system. By the late 1920s, much of northern Louisiana's pine forests had been completely destroyed for their timber. The government bought some of the logged land and allowed cypress and pine trees to grow back. Hard work by the Forest Service has restored the landscape for wildlife and built trails for hikers and bikers.

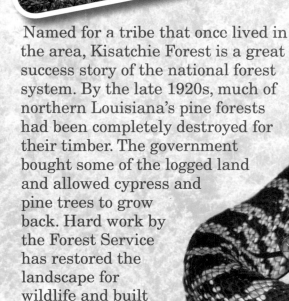

BLUE RIDGE

Parkway

Year of Quarter: 2015
Location of Park: North Carolina and Virginia
Date of Park's Founding: 1936
Approximate Park Area: 95,000 acres
Fun Fact: The Blue Ridge Music Center is one of the only places in a national park dedicated to local music performance and history.

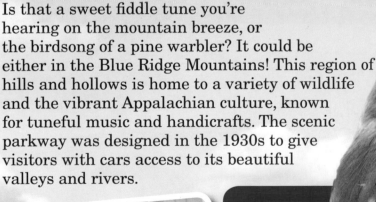

A drive along the Blue Ridge Parkway is beautiful in the fall, but be sure to stop at the Blue Ridge Music Center (bottom left).

Is that a sweet fiddle tune you're hearing on the mountain breeze, or the birdsong of a pine warbler? It could be either in the Blue Ridge Mountains! This region of hills and hollows is home to a variety of wildlife and the vibrant Appalachian culture, known for tuneful music and handicrafts. The scenic parkway was designed in the 1930s to give visitors with cars access to its beautiful valleys and rivers.

Saw-whet owl

BOMBAY HOOK

National Wildlife Refuge

Year of Quarter: 2015
Location of Park: Delaware
Date of Park's Founding: 1937
Approximate Park Area: 16,000 acres
Fun Fact: The name of the park has nothing to do with the city of Bombay (now Mumbai), India. It comes from the Dutch words *bompies hoeck*, which mean "little tree point."

Careful and quiet birdwatchers can see as many as 275 different species of birds that visit the refuge each year, including the black-crowned night heron (below).

Like a rest stop for drivers on a highway, the saltwater marshland of Bombay Hook is an essential stopping-off place for **migrating** birds, where they can rest and eat in safety. Flocks of geese and ducks as well as thousands of tiny songbirds stop here every spring and fall. The national wildlife **refuge** network keeps these key areas safe for animals that need them.

SARATOGA

National Historical Park

Year of Quarter: 2015

Location of Park: New York

Date of Park's Founding: 1927 (as New York State Historical Preserve); 1938 as National Historical Park

Approximate Park Area: 3,400 acres

Fun Fact: The Boot Monument is a tribute to American Major General Benedict Arnold's leadership, but because Arnold later fought for the British, his name is not on the memorial!

The small red Neilson farmhouse, right, was built just before the Revolutionary War broke out.

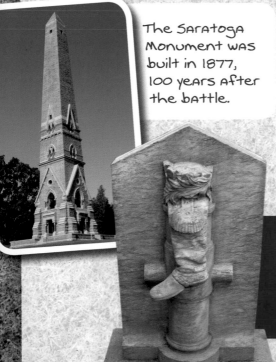

The Saratoga Monument was built in 1877, 100 years after the battle.

This park is made up of four sites important to the history of the Battle of Saratoga, a multi-day conflict in October 1777 between the rebel American forces and the British troops of General John "Gentleman Johnny" Burgoyne. When the Americans accepted his surrender, it was a big morale boost for their cause. Fun events are held year-round to teach about life during the Revolutionary War era.

The nameless "boot monument" to turncoat Benedict Arnold (1741–1801)

SHAWNEE

National Forest

Year of Quarter: 2016
Location of Park: Illinois
Date of Park's Founding: 1939
Approximate Park Area: 280,000 acres
Fun Fact: The forest's limestone bluffs are mentioned in the journal of explorer Meriwether Lewis, who passed through it in November 1803 on his trip to the Pacific Ocean.

Worn down by wind and rain, these knobby sandstone rocks are known as the Garden of the Gods.

Explorer Meriwether Lewis, 1774–1809

Visitors to Shawnee Forest in southern Illinois enjoy the same creeks and limestone bluffs that Native Americans lived among for thousands of years. National forest workers maintain the leafy forest's diverse habitats with careful pruning, tree felling, and even controlled burns of limited areas. They also work hard to keep out **invasive species**, both animals and plants, which could disrupt the balance of wildlife.

A controlled forest burn

CUMBERLAND GAP

National Historical Park

Year of Quarter: 2016
Location of Park: Kentucky, Tennessee, and Virginia
Date of Park's Founding: 1940
Approximate Park Area: 24,000 acres
Fun Fact: The Cumberland Gap and Cumberland Island in Georgia (see page 49) were both named in the 1700s for Prince William, Duke of Cumberland, whose father, King George II, ruled England and the American colonies at the time.

Bridging three states, the Gap has hilly scenic overlooks and underground caves.

The Cumberland Gap is an opening in heavily wooded hills where hunters, explorers, and settlers could take a shortcut to the western lands beyond. For centuries, it was part of the Warriors' Path used by the Shawnee and Cherokee. In the 1700s, woodsman Daniel Boone led many settlers into the area. Violent conflicts over who controlled the Gap broke out during Lord Dunmore's War (1774), the Revolutionary War (1776–1783), and the Civil War (1860–1865).

Split-rail fences and the historic iron furnace

Trailblazer Daniel Boone (1734–1820)

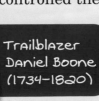

HARPERS FERRY

National Historical Park

Year of Quarter: 2016
Location of Park: West Virginia, Virginia, and Maryland
Date of Park's Founding: 1944
Approximate Park Area: 3,700 acres
Fun Fact: Because the corners of three states meet within the park lands, you can hike through three different states in one day!

Radical abolitionist John Brown (1800–1859) tried to take control of army supplies at Harper's Ferry in July 1859, just before the Civil War. He was arrested at "John Brown's Fort" (lower right).

Step back in time to the 1860s, when this town at the junction of the Potomac and Shenandoah Rivers was a powder keg of tensions between the North and South. A farm, school, blacksmith, and several shops are all run as they would have been a hundred and fifty years ago. Many famous people from American history have connections with Harpers Ferry, including Thomas Jefferson, General Thomas "Stonewall" Jackson, and educator W. E. B. DuBois.

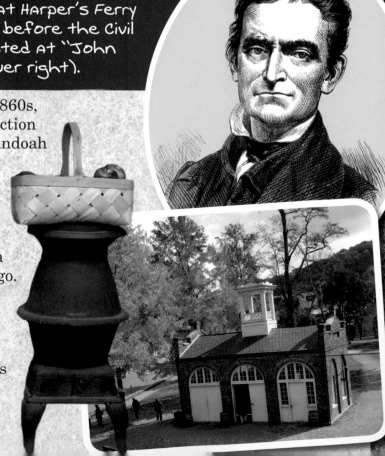

THEODORE ROOSEVELT

National Park

Year of Quarter: 2016
Location of Park: North Dakota
Date of Park's Founding: 1946 (as Theodore Roosevelt National Wildlife Refuge); 1978 renamed and expanded
Approximate Park Area: 70,000 acres
Fun Fact: Presidents Teddy Roosevelt and Abraham Lincoln tie for the most national park sites that contain their names or homes—five each.

The wild horses that live within the park are descended from tame horses brought by Spanish explorers hundreds of years ago. Prairie dogs (upper left) also live in the park.

America's 26th president, Theodore "Teddy" Roosevelt, preferred the great outdoors to the inside of the White House. Before becoming president, he owned a ranch in the North Dakota Badlands and loved riding horses and hiking there. Making these lands into a national park was a fitting way to honor his contributions to **conservation** in America. Although rough weather and a rocky landscape have given this region the nickname "Badlands," many animals thrive here.

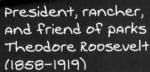

President, rancher, and friend of parks Theodore Roosevelt (1858–1919)

FORT MOULTRIE

(Fort Sumter National Monument)

Year of Quarter: 2016
Location of Park: South Carolina
Date of Park's Founding: 1948
Approximate Park Area: 240 acres
Fun Fact: When British forces controlled Charleston from 1780 to 1782, Fort Moultrie was called Fort Arbuthnot.

Weapons and defensive walls at Fort Moultrie show the history of many conflicts that reached Charleston Harbor.

Visitors to Fort Sumter, the starting place of the Civil War, can take a ferry to nearby Sullivan's Island and learn about the many roles Fort Moultrie has played in American history. Unlike Fort Sumter, which was built in the 1850s, Fort Moultrie was in use since the Revolutionary War, and has been rebuilt three times. It saw battles and hosted training and housing facilities for the U.S. Army from 1776 to 1947.

EFFIGY MOUNDS

National Monument

Year of Quarter: 2017
Location of Park: Iowa
Date of Park's Founding: 1949
Approximate Park Area: 2,500 acres
Fun Fact: Mound shapes may include bison, birds, bear, and turtles — but no horses, which didn't live in North America until Europeans brought them by ship.

Viewed from above, the outlines of many animals seem to be marching across the landscape.

Have you ever molded wet sand at the beach into an animal shape? The Effigy Mounds are shapes of bears and birds sculpted out of the ground by an ancient Native American culture. This national monument area is considered holy ground by 12 modern-day tribes; other visitors are encouraged to respectfully enjoy these mysterious and beautiful earthworks in the wooded Upper Mississippi landscape.

The Mississippi River flows past the monument.

Exhibits at the visitor center show the natural and human history of the area.

FREDERICK DOUGLASS

National Historic Site

Year of Quarter: 2017

Location of Park: District of Columbia (Washington, DC)

Date of Park's Founding: 1900 (as Frederick Douglass Memorial and Historical Association); 1962 as National Historic Site

Approximate Park Area: 8 acres

Fun Fact: Douglass called the small building he used for writing his "growlery," because writing and thinking made him cranky!

Many of Frederick Douglass's (1818–1895) most treasured possessions, such as his books and writing desk, are preserved in the house.

Frederick Douglass was born a slave in Maryland in 1818, but he escaped and became one of the leading antislavery speakers and writers of the pre–Civil War period, traveling around the northern states and to Europe. In 1878, he settled in Washington, DC, at a house named Cedar Hill, and continued to write and speak for the rights of all Americans until his death in 1895. Visitors to Cedar Hill can see what life was like for his family in the late 1800s.

Elegant Cedar Hill was a stylish home of the 1800s.

OZARK

National Scenic Riverways

Year of Quarter: 2017
Location of Park: Missouri
Date of Park's Founding: 1964
Approximate Park Area: 81,000 acres
Fun Fact: Big Spring lets out over 286 million gallons of water a day, enough to fill a football stadium!

Built in 1894, the big red Alley Mill used water power to grind grain into flour.

Unlike most rivers, whose water comes from melting snow and rainfall, the Jacks Forks and Current Rivers are fed by underground cold springs. Mostly underlaid by limestone, this area is full of caves, springs, and sinkholes. In 2011, rangers closed the caves to human visitors to protect the bats that live there from disease.

Ozark National Scenic Riverways is the first national park area to protect a wild river system.

ELLIS ISLAND

Statue of Liberty National Monument

Year of Quarter: 2017

Location of Park: New Jersey and New York

Date of Park's Founding: 1965

Approximate Park Area: 61 acres

Fun Fact: Over 17 million immigrants passed through Ellis Island between 1892 and 1924.

The dirt and rocks used as filler to enlarge Ellis Island came from the tunnels dug for the New York City subway!

The Statue of Liberty

One of the most recognizable symbols of the United States is the Statue of Liberty, which greets arrivals to New York Harbor. On nearby Ellis Island, the former immigration processing building now holds fascinating exhibits about the millions of people who came from around the world to make America their home.

Immigrants were processed in the Great Hall.

George Rogers Clark

National Historical Park

Year of Quarter: 2017
Location of Park: Indiana
Date of Park's Founding: 1966
Approximate Park Area: 26 acres
Fun Fact: Clark fooled the British troops into thinking he had more soldiers than he did by waving many flags and lighting explosives to make a lot of noise!

Italian-born merchant Francis Vigo (a statue in his honor, upper left, 1747–1836) assisted Clark's raid with supplies and information. Inside the round stone memorial to Lieutenant George Rogers Clark (left, 1752–1819) are paintings showing his daring winter campaign against the British.

This peaceful site along the Ohio River saw a turning point of the Revolutionary War. In a daring raid on Fort Sackville in the winter of 1779, Lieutenant Colonel George Rogers Clark captured the fort from the British and so took control of the western frontier for the Americans.

The fort is long gone, but local pride in Clark's victory remained, and a memorial to Clark's bravery and leadership was built on the site in the 1930s.

PICTURED ROCKS

National Lakeshore

Year of Quarter: 2018
Location of Park: Michigan
Date of Park's Founding: 1966
Approximate Park Area: 73,000 acres
Fun Fact: The signal beam from the Au Sable Light Station, built in 1874, could be seen up to 18 miles out in Lake Superior.

The Au Sable (French for "with sand") lighthouse and foghorn, built in 1874, were maintained by a team of workers who lived next door, warning ships of bad weather 24 hours a day.

Along the southern shore of Lake Superior, the largest of the five Great Lakes, waves have carved out caves and rock formations into the multicolored sandstone cliffs, inspiring the name Pictured Rocks. Once a major route for shipping, the lakeshore is still dotted with historic lighthouses and Coast Guard stations. Visitors can enjoy this park by hiking along the cliffs or boating in the lake.

Chapel Rock

Visitors can stroll 42 miles of protected lakeshore.

APOSTLE ISLANDS

National Lakeshore

Year of Quarter: 2018
Location of Park: Wisconsin
Date of Park's Founding: 1970
Approximate Park Area: 69,000 acres
Fun Fact: Apostle Islands has six lighthouses—more than any other national park site!

Boaters in all kinds of craft enjoy the scenic waters and islands of Lake Superior.

The historic home of the Ojibwe people, the Apostle Islands of Lake Superior were named and mapped by French missionaries in the 1700s. This national lakeshore is made up of 21 islands and 12 miles of mainland coast. Some islands are reserved for nesting birds or those making a migration stopoff, including endangered species; others welcome human visitors, who may arrive by motorboat, sailboat, and kayak.

Long Island Light Tower

VOYAGEURS

National Park

Year of Quarter: 2018
Location of Park: Minnesota
Date of Park's Founding: 1975
Approximate Park Area: 220,000 acres
Fun Fact: A miniature gold rush began around the park's Little American Island in 1893, but only one site turned out to have any gold.

Beavers (upper right) live in areas with many lakes and streams, so fur trappers targeted this area in the 1700s and 1800s.

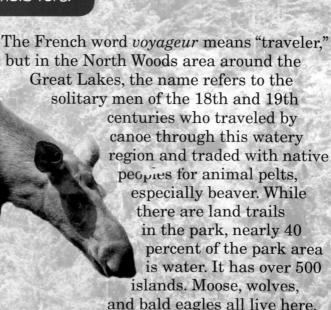

The voyageurs braved tough conditions in search of valuable furs.

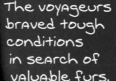

The French word *voyageur* means "traveler," but in the North Woods area around the Great Lakes, the name refers to the solitary men of the 18th and 19th centuries who traveled by canoe through this watery region and traded with native peoples for animal pelts, especially beaver. While there are land trails in the park, nearly 40 percent of the park area is water. It has over 500 islands. Moose, wolves, and bald eagles all live here.

CUMBERLAND ISLAND

National Seashore

Year of Quarter: 2018
Location of Park: Georgia
Date of Park's Founding: 1972
Approximate Park Area: 36,000 acres
Fun Fact: A Spanish **mission** settlement on the island was attacked by pirates in 1683 and 1684, eventually driving off the missionaries.

Lovely Plum Orchard Mansion (left), built in 1898, is open to tours, while only ruins remain of Dungeness House (lower right, with a wild horse). The historic First African Baptist Church (bottom right) can also be visited.

Many different groups have settled on this island off of Georgia over time, from Spanish missionaries in the 1600s to the wealthy Carnegie family in the 20th century. Today most of the island is left wild. The protected shores are an important nesting site for sea turtles. Manatees and sharks also swim around the shore, and wild horses, armadillos, and bobcats live in the protected interior.

BLOCK ISLAND

National Wildlife Refuge

Year of Quarter: 2018
Location of Park: Rhode Island
Date of Park's Founding: 1973
Approximate Park Area: 133 acres
Fun Fact: Some species of voles, frogs, and snakes on Block Island may be unique in the entire world, because they have been separated from mainland animals for so long.

Because of efforts at the refuge to protect their nests, the population of piping plovers (lower left) is increasing.

A teardrop-shaped island in the Atlantic Ocean, Block Island is an important landmark on the migration route used by millions of birds that fly south for the winter. This small wildlife refuge protects an area of shoreline and ponds where migrating songbirds can rest. Scientists keep track of the bird traffic by watching, counting, and sometimes banding the birds—putting a numbered ID tag on one leg so they can track their progress.

LOWELL
National Historical Park

Year of Quarter: 2019
Location of Park: Massachusetts
Date of Park's Founding: 1978
Approximate Park Area: 140 acres
Fun Fact: Visitors can tour Lowell's historic sites by trolley and canal boat.

The water-powered machine looms at Lowell were the latest technology in the 19th century.

Some of the old machines are kept working for display purposes.

Clang! Clang! went the bells of Lowell, waking up mill workers at 4:30 A.M., six days a week, and giving the signal for meals and shift changes that could be heard all over town. Built on the Merrimack River in the 1820s, Lowell was the first planned factory city in America, and used water power from canals to drive power looms for weaving cloth. Staffed mostly by women and immigrants, the mills are a landmark of the Industrial Revolution.

AMERICAN

Memorial Park

Year of Quarter: 2019
Location of Park: Saipan, Northern Mariana Islands (a U.S. territory in the Pacific Ocean)
Date of Park's Founding: 1978
Approximate Park Area: 130 acres
Fun Fact: Watch out for the huge coconut crab, a land crustacean that can grow 12 inches wide!

The park's dramatic scenery can be explored on foot or underwater.

When the United States entered World War II on December 7, 1941, four years of conflict by air and sea began. The war in the Pacific claimed thousands of lives, many of which are remembered at a Court of Honor on the island of Saipan, now part of the U.S. territory of the Mariana Islands. The park also hosts the annual Flame Tree Festival, celebrating Pacific Island music, dance, and culture.

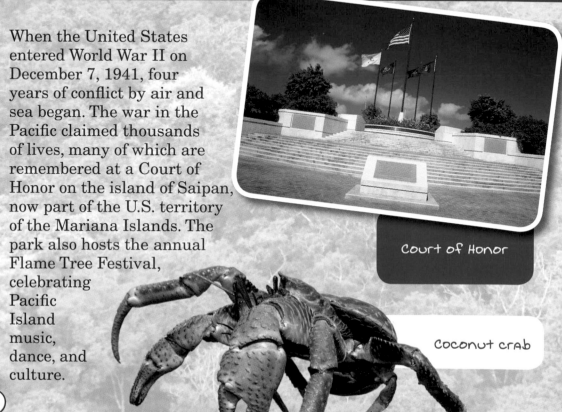

Court of Honor

Coconut crab

WAR IN THE PACIFIC

National Historical Park

Year of Quarter: 2019
Location of Park: Guam (a U.S. territory island in the Pacific Ocean)
Date of Park's Founding: 1978
Approximate Park Area: 2,000 acres
Fun Fact: In addition to its historic sites, the park also includes coral reefs where visitors can snorkel and scuba dive.

Sunset at Apaca Point. The peaceful waters and islands of the Pacific saw many years of fighting during World War II.

A scuba diver explores the reef.

Three days after the Japanese attack on Pearl Harbor, Hawaii, Japan invaded and occupied another U.S. territory, the island of Guam. Japan held it until it was fully retaken by U.S. marines and army troops on July 21, 1944. Several places associated with the occupation and the Pacific conflict make up Guam's park today. The island is peaceful now, but still at the mercy of typhoons, one of which destroyed the park's visitor center in 2007.

SAN ANTONIO MISSIONS

National Historical Park

Year of Quarter: 2019
Location of Park: Texas
Date of Park's Founding: 1978
Approximate Park Area: 830 acres
Fun Fact: Two hundred years before car travel, a highway called El Camino Real de los Tejas, or the Royal Road of Texas, stretched 1,000 miles between Mexico City and present-day Louisiana.

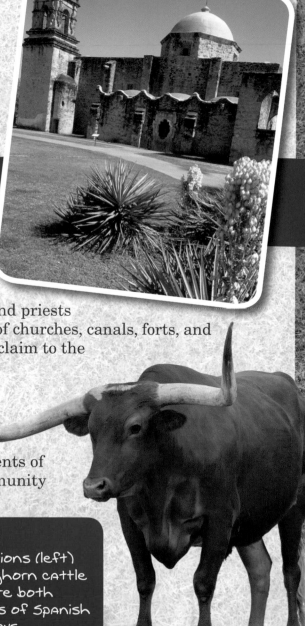

Mission San José (right) was the largest in the area, with thriving farms and a ranch in the late 1700s.

The Texas city of San Antonio got its start in Spanish colonial days. Beginning in 1718, soldiers and priests from Spain established a network of churches, canals, forts, and farms in this area to boost Spain's claim to the land. The San Antonio Missions park includes four mission complexes, which both show what life was like in the Spanish-speaking mission settlements of the 1700s, and are active community centers today.

Colorful decorations (left) and longhorn cattle (right) are both reminders of Spanish colonial days.

FRANK CHURCH–RIVER OF NO RETURN

Wilderness

Year of Quarter: 2019
Location of Park: Idaho
Date of Park's Founding: 1980
Approximate Park Area: 2,400,000 acres
Fun Fact: The canyon of the Middle Fork of the Salmon River is 6,300 feet deep — even deeper than the Grand Canyon on the Colorado River.

The challenging rapids of the Salmon River are a thrill for rafters.

Senator and conservation advocate Frank Church (1924–1984)

In 1964, the Wilderness Act became law, allowing for large pieces of land to remain untouched and wild. Unlike national parks, which usually have many paved roads and conveniences for visitors, these lands are left as they were found for wildlife, and for outdoor adventurers who enjoy a challenge. A major supporter of the **Wilderness Act**, Senator Frank Church, is remembered in the name of one of the nation's largest wilderness areas, found in his home state of Idaho.

National Park of
AMERICAN SAMOA

Year of Quarter: 2020
Location of Park: American Samoa
(a U.S. territory island in the Pacific Ocean)
Date of Park's Founding: 1988
Approximate Park Area: 14,000 acres
Fun Fact: The park's endangered flying fox is actually a giant bat. It eats only fruit.

The islands rise dramatically out of the sea as the highest points of an underwater volcanic ridge.

The National Park Service manages land on three of this small territory's five islands plus two atolls: Tutuila, Ofu, and Ta'u. Visitors who make the long trip over the Pacific Ocean find a beautiful and dramatic landscape, with soaring green mountains rising above the beaches and an undersea world of brightly colored fish and coral. Rather than staying in hotels, visitors are encouraged to lodge with a native Samoan family.

The small Samoan islands have few native animals, but a great variety of sea life thrives in the warm ocean waters around them.

WEIR FARM

National Historic Site

Year of Quarter: 2020
Location of Park: Connecticut
Date of Park's Founding: 1990
Approximate Park Area: 74 acres
Fun Fact: Weir Farm is the only national historic site that preserves the home of a painter.

The pleasant scenery of Weir Farm charmed its owners and visitors.

Many parks inspire visitors to create beautiful photographs, drawings, and paintings; at this farm 60 miles north of New York City, paintings inspired the creation of a park! In 1882, painter and art dealer J. Alden Weir traded a painting for a pretty Connecticut farmhouse and its land. While they lived there, Weir and his family were charmed by the gentle landscape, and many famous artists came to visit. Now the Weirs' farm inspires more visitors than ever!

Many of today's visitors also make art.

Large windows helped convert a barn into a studio.

57

SALT RIVER BAY

National Historical Park and Ecological Preserve

Year of Quarter: 2020
Location of Park: St. Croix, U.S. Virgin Islands (a U.S. territory in the Caribbean Sea)
Date of Park's Founding: 1992
Approximate Park Area: 990 acres
Fun Fact: The park contains the ruins of an ancient ball court, called a *batey*, for a Taino game believed similar to basketball.

An artist's portrait of Christopher Columbus

The island of St. Croix in the Caribbean Sea has seen many cultures come and go: Igneri, Taino, and Carib societies each had their time on the island, and Spanish, English, French, and Dutch colonists also claimed it. Since 1917, the island has been owned by the United States. Salt River Park shows the island's many layers of history, and has trails for hiking and beaches for swimming and snorkeling.

A windmill used to press sugarcane, a key crop of the island

MARSH-BILLINGS-ROCKEFELLER

National Historical Park

Year of Quarter: 2020
Location of Park: Vermont
Date of Park's Founding: 1992
Approximate Park Area: 640 acres
Fun Fact: Laurance Rockefeller, the property's last private owner, was the first person to be awarded the Congressional Gold Medal for work with conservation.

The beautiful Vermont scenery surrounds visitors with the rewards of conservation.

The mansion exhibits many landscape paintings.

Three generations of families with progressive ideas about preserving America's amazing wild places lived in the same house in Vermont's Green Mountains, making it the perfect place for a park permanently dedicated to the history of conservation in the United States. The benefits of saving forests to enjoy are all around you here. The hilly woodland area is great for strolling, hiking, or snowshoeing.

TALLGRASS PRAIRIE

National Preserve

Year of Quarter: 2020
Location of Park: Kansas
Date of Park's Founding: 1996
Approximate Park Area: 11,000 acres
Fun Fact: Occasional fires are necessary to clear out dead plants and maintain the prairie ecosystem in a place like Tallgrass. Fires can be naturally started by lightning.

The tall grass is very good for livestock, and cows still graze the land where buffalo once roamed.

1881 Spring Hill Ranch house

The habitat called tallgrass prairie used to cover 140 million acres of North America, but almost all of it has been plowed under for farms and ranches. This site in Kansas shows what the prairie looked like until homesteading in the 1800s (see page 31). Many animals and birds live in the tall grassland, and special events throughout the year show what life was like for early farmers in the area.

TUSKEGEE AIRMEN

National Historic Site

Year of Quarter: 2021
Location of Park: Alabama
Date of Park's Founding: 1998
Approximate Park Area: 90 acres
Fun Fact: Historic aviation shows are held twice a year on Moton Field, showing daring maneuvers with aircraft like the original Tuskegee pilots used.

Many heroes of World War II came from the Tuskegee flight training program.

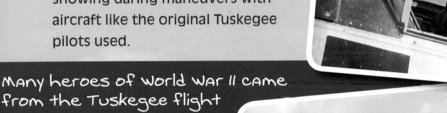

An aircraft control tower at Moton Field

Founded in 1881, the Tuskegee Institute provided a college education for black students at a time when they were often not welcome at other universities. Unfair rules also applied in the military, but by the 1930s, military leaders could no longer deny brave Americans of all races the right to defend their country from the air. The Tuskegee site tells the story of the first African American pilots, mechanics, navigators, and support staff who were trained there.

1. **Hot Spring National Park (Arkansas):** 2010
2. **Yellowstone National Park (Wyoming):** 2010
3. **Yosemite National Park (California):** 2010
4. **Grand Canyon National Park (Arizona):** 2010
5. **Mt. Hood National Forest (Oregon):** 2010
6. **Gettysburg National Military Park (Pennsylvania):** 2011
7. **Glacier National Park (Montana):** 2011
8. **Olympic National Park (Washington):** 2011
9. **Vicksburg National Military Park (Mississippi):** 2011
10. **Chickasaw National Recreation Area (Oklahoma):** 2011
11. **El Yunque National Forest (Puerto Rico):** 2012
12. **Chaco Culture National Historical Park (New Mexico):** 2012
13. **Acadia National Park (Maine):** 2012
14. **Hawai'i Volcanoes National Park (Hawaii):** 2012
15. **Denali National Park (Alaska):** 2012
16. **White Mountain National Forest (New Hampshire):** 2013
17. **Perry's Victory and International Peace Memorial (Ohio):** 2013

18. **Great Basin National Park (Nevada):** 2013
19. **Fort McHenry National Monument and Historic Shrine (Maryland):** 2013
20. **Mount Rushmore National Memorial (South Dakota):** 2013
21. **Great Smoky Mountains National Park (Tennessee):** 2014
22. **Shenandoah National Park (Virginia):** 2014
23. **Arches National Park (Utah):** 2014
24. **Great Sand Dunes National Park (Colorado):** 2014
25. **Everglades National Park (Florida):** 2014
26. **Homestead National Monument of America (Nebraska):** 2015
27. **Kisatchie National Forest (Louisiana):** 2015
28. **Blue Ridge Parkway (North Carolina):** 2015
29. **Bombay Hook National Wildlife Refuge (Delaware):** 2015
30. **Saratoga National Historical Park (New York):** 2015
31. **Shawnee National Forest (Illinois):** 2016

NATIONAL PARKS MAP

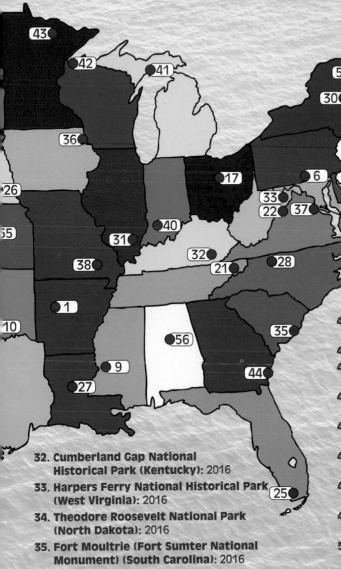

32. **Cumberland Gap National Historical Park (Kentucky):** 2016

33. **Harpers Ferry National Historical Park (West Virginia):** 2016

34. **Theodore Roosevelt National Park (North Dakota):** 2016

35. **Fort Moultrie (Fort Sumter National Monument) (South Carolina):** 2016

36. **Effigy Mounds National Monument (Iowa):** 2017

37. **Frederick Douglass National Historic Site (District of Columbia):** 2017

38. **Ozark National Scenic Riverways (Missouri):** 2017

39. **Ellis Island (Statue of Liberty National Monument) (New Jersey):** 2017

40. **George Rogers Clark National Historical Park (Indiana):** 2017

41. **Pictured Rocks National Lakeshore (Michigan):** 2018

42. **Apostle Islands National Lakeshore (Wisconsin):** 2018

43. **Voyageurs National Park (Minnesota):** 2018

44. **Cumberland Island National Seashore (Georgia):** 2018

45. **Block Island National Wildlife Refuge (Rhode Island):** 2018

46. **Lowell National Historical Park (Massachusetts):** 2019

47. **American Memorial Park (Northern Mariana Islands):** 2019

48. **War in the Pacific National Historical Park (Guam):** 2019

49. **San Antonio Missions National Historical Park (Texas):** 2019

50. **Frank Church–River of No Return Wilderness (Idaho):** 2019

51. **National Park of American Samoa (American Samoa):** 2020

52. **Weir Farm National Historic Site (Connecticut):** 2020

53. **Salt River Bay National Historical Park and Ecological Preserve (U.S. Virgin Islands):** 2020

54. **Marsh-Billings-Rockefeller National Historical Park (Vermont):** 2020

55. **Tallgrass Prairie National Preserve (Kansas):** 2020

56. **Tuskegee Airmen National Historic Site (Alabama):** 2021

GLOSSARY

Civilian Conservation Corps (CCC): a federal jobs program (1933–1942) that hired unemployed workers to help improve national park lands and forests.

conservation: the practice of protecting natural areas or living things from damage by humans.

ecosystem: the group of animals and plants who naturally live in a certain area and are in balance with one another.

geyser: a heated jet of water that is ejected out of the ground, often very high into the air, by the force of underground pressure.

homestead: a house and farm built on previously unoccupied land, especially in response to the 1862 Homestead Act, which gave land to those who farmed it.

ice age: prehistoric times, lasting millions of years, when the Earth's temperature was so cold that much of the land mass was covered with glaciers.

invasive species: a plant or animal, often moved by humans, that is so successful living in a new region that it harms the wildlife already living there.

migration: the act of moving to another place to live because conditions are better, especially better weather.

National Park Service: the U.S. federal agency that manages all national parks and many other protected areas.

mission: in the 1700s, a walled community with a church, garden, living areas, and other buildings built by Spanish priests to promote the Catholic religion and Spanish customs in the Americas.

park ranger: a person employed to maintain the parks' trails and campgrounds and monitor such threats as forest fires and invasive species.

refuge: a protected place. In this context, an area set aside to conserve wildlife.

sequoia: a very tall type of tree with cones and needles.

siege: a military tactic in which an enemy area is cut off from supplies or attacked until it surrenders.

U.S. Mint: the U.S. agency that makes all coins. It was created by Congress in 1792.

watershed: a large area where rainfall or icemelt gathers that feeds into a river or other body of water.

Weeks Act: 1911 law that established the national forest system.

Wilderness Act: 1964 law that established the National Wilderness system.